I0120952

Table of Contents

The Skillful Questioner 2

Making Questions Powerful 6

How to Use This Book..8

Additional Uses 10

Open and Closed-Ended Questions Chart 13

General Career Transition Questions...14

Career Transition Wheel 46

Passion Questions 47

Innate Talent Questions..48

Transferable Skills Questions...49

Work Experience Questions...51

Accomplishment Questions...53

Core Values Questions 54

Self-Expression Questions 57

Lifestyle Questions..59

Career Values / Quality Assessment...63

Blank Wheel 65

Career Quotes 66

SMART Goals Checklist..71

About the Work 72

About the Authors 73

Additional Valuable Resources 74

The Skillful Questioner

Problems cannot be solved by the same level of thinking that created them.
   ~ Albert Einstein

During the Renaissance there was a massive resurgence of learning and a gradual yet widespread shift in education, leading to economic growth and development, political and social reform, and an increase in trade and commerce.

The Industrial Revolution was a major turning point in human history. There were immense technological advancements, economic progress, income & population growth, and an increase in the standard of living never seen before.

Why?

They were asking themselves powerful questions that shifted the way they approached problems, and spurred curiosity and creativity.

Today, we are on the verge of another major shift. To make the leap we need to make we must ask ourselves and our clients questions that achieve & surpass that same level of curiosity and creativity.

The quality of questions we ask directly influence the knowledge we acquire and the actions we take.

By asking quality, empowering questions we can find the answers leading to the change we seek.

Being a skillful questioner is more than just the words used in the questions. It's as much about how you ask the questions as it is about the words you use. Having no attachment to the outcome of the question and addressing the questioner with curiosity, objectivity and in a non- confrontational manner creates an atmosphere of safety for the questionee to answer honestly and thoroughly.

With over 30 years of coaching, training, facilitation, and experiential learning experience between the two of them, both Denny & Kathy Jo recognize even the most skilled professionals can sometimes get stuck finding the right questions.

Asking powerful questions allow the questionee to see things differently, open up creativity, gain new perspectives, see solutions, discover their own answers, deepens relationships and trust, and improves problem-solving and decision-making abilities.

You can ask the most empowering questions and unlock amazing possibilities, but unless you truly listen and the questionee feels that intent, forward movement is stunted. Listening is an important part of communication as is asking powerful questions. However, not all listening is effective listening.

It is said that hearing is a physical ability. We all hear. We don't always listen. Listening is a skill, one that must be practiced and intentional to be effective.

As a vital part of the questioning process, listening enables:
- The acquisition of new information
- Greater insight to the values, strengths, behavior and needs of the questionee
- The questionee to discover his / her own perspectives of the situation
- Trust & Rapport
- Understanding of underlying meaning
- Motivation
- Depth & Intimacy
- Mutual understanding
- The questionee to feel heard and understood

Levels of Listening

There are 4 Levels of Listening. We have all experienced listening to others and being listened to at each level. The higher the level the more energy is required to maintain that level. Not every conversation you have will take place at the Intuitive Listening level.

1. **Competitive Listening**: The main focus in Competitive Listening is on the listener's own thoughts. Here the listener is more interested in their own views and is waiting for an opportunity to jump in and react.

2. **Attentive Listening**: The main focus in Attentive Listening is on the words being said. There is genuine interest in hearing and understanding what is being said but assumes that understanding, not checking with the questionee for confirmation.

3. **Reflective Listening**: The main focus in Reflective Listening is on a deeper and clarified understanding of what is being said. There is genuine interest in listening and understanding what is being said and confirms that understanding, often through mirroring back the exact information shared.

4. **Intuitive Listening**: The main focus on Intuitive Listening is an understanding of the meaning of what is being said. There is genuine desire to understand not only the meaning of what is being said but also the tone, pitch, speed, of what's being said, the body language that accompanies the words, what is being said behind the words and what is NOT being said.

We all know how important communication is. However, the vast majority of communication isn't spoken. According to studies done in the '70s by Albert Mehrabian, only 7% of communication takes place through exchange of words. The remaining 93% of information is communicated through body language, eye contact, and pitch, speed, tone and volume of the voice.

Understanding that most information is not communicated through words, to be a powerful listener there are several things you have to keep in mind while listening to the questionee.

Keys to Powerful Listening

1. Intentions are set to gain a greater understanding of the questionee, their behavior, thinking, values, beliefs, perspectives and needs.
2. Stay Curious.
3. Detached Involvement: the ability to tap into deep levels of empathy and place yourself in the questionees position, understanding their thoughts and feelings without taking on their emotions.
4. Focus on what is being communicated in all areas – body language, tone, pace, pitch, energy – while not focusing on how you would like to respond.
5. Offer feedback and request clarification if necessary.
6. Remember silence is golden. Don't be afraid of silence, allow the questionee to sit with the question and ponder.
7. Use Intuitive Listening as much as possible.

When entering a conversation where you are required to deeply listen and understand questionees, try your best to enter the situation with as much energy as possible.

Powerful Questions + Intuitive Listening + Acknowledgement + Time to Respond = Unlocked Potential & Possibilities

Making Questions Powerful

Asking the right questions in the right way is key to achieving the right results. Powerful questions immediately access our creative, holistic brain from which solutions are born. These thought provoking questions are designed to forward your client's actions through clarifying, inspiring, probing, challenging, affirming, exploring, opening new possibilities, connecting, assessing, and evaluating, leading to the right solutions for your client.

When crafting questions, there are 3 things you must consider.
1. The Scope of the Question
2. The Construction of the Question
3. Assumptions & Bias in the Question

Scope

The Scope is defined as the range or subject matter that something deals with or to which it is relevant. The scope covers the domain of inquiry. Matching the scope of the question to meet the needs of inquiry increases the capacity to effect change and sets the questionee up for success. Therefore, keep within realistic boundaries of the situation and questionee's knowledge and power.

For example: "How can you best change your perspective?" as opposed to "How can you change the perspective within the organization?"

When determining the scope of your question you must first determine the scope of the answer you are seeking. If you are looking for greater clarification you must ask questions designed to gain clarity. If you are looking for greater insight, you must ask questions designed to go deeper. If you are looking at obstacles you must ask questions designed to uncover blocks. The scope of the answer determines the category of the question to achieve an appropriate response. You can find the question categories under the General Questions section of this book.

Construction

The construction of a question consists of the language, intention and tone you take when asking the question. A question's construction is a critical element in either opening up one's mind to possibilities or closing the mind to solutions. The construction of a question can determine the depth and direction of the answers. Are you looking for a direct yes or no answer? Ask a closed-ended question. Are you looking for deeper clarification? Do you want to open choices or create a new picture? Ask open-ended questions.

The construction of a question stimulates reflective thinking and deepens the conversation. Starting your question with either "who" or "how" determines the level and direction of inquiry. For example: "Who can help you to make this happen?" "How can this happen?"

When constructing the question, ask yourself what "work" you want this question to do.

Assumptions and Bias

Part of being human is that our experiences and perspectives influence the way we think. We all carry with us assumptions and biases. We cannot eliminate them. Awareness of assumptions and biases allow us to be on the look-out for them as we construct and ask our questions, and listen to the answer.

One of the most commonly used questions containing an assumption or bias is "What is wrong?" This question assumes a negative.

Reframing is a potent way to reword questions freeing them of assumptions and bias such as from "What's wrong?" to "What happened?" Reframing encourages deeper reflection and shifts assumptions into possibilities for creating forward action.

A Word About "Why"

Some of the most powerful questions begin with "Why." Some of the most dangerous questions begin with "Why."

Why-questions can lead to greater insight and more thorough answers. They ask the questionee to go deeper and evaluate. Answers to why-questions speak about the inner feelings, beliefs, and motives of the questionee. Because of the highly personal nature of why-questions safety and trust must be established in the relationship. If not, a why-question can easily trigger reactive behaviors and blame leading detracting from solutions.

The difference between getting greater insight and triggering reaction is the level of safety the questionee feels in the relationship and the way in which the question is asked.

If safety and trust have been established on both sides of the relationship and a why-question is the most appropriate question to ask, stay curious when asking your question. This will keep the non-verbal elements of asking a question as well as your intention on maintaining safety and trust and away from blame.

Choose why-questions carefully and sparingly.

Characteristics of a Powerful Question

1. Solutions-focused
2. Clear & Simple
3. Involves Values & Ideals
4. Generates Curiosity
5. Stimulates Reflection
6. Thought-Provoking
7. Engages Attention
8. Focused
9. Touches Deeper Meaning
10. Leads to More Questions

How to Use This Book?

As you encounter a specific challenge around Career Transitions in your life or your client's life, you may become stuck and not know where to go next. This book is designed to assist in getting you and your clients unstuck by sparking new, unique, and in-depth questions. You can either use these questions as is or allow them to inspire new ideas for you.

Open / Closed-Ended Questions Chart: Open-Ended questions are designed to require the answerer to go deeper and give more detail. These types of questions should be used as often as possible to gain greater detail, inquiry, and increase understanding. Closed-Ended questions are excellent for commitment. These are used ONLY when looking for a "yes" or "no" response.

General Career Questions: These general Career Transition-based questions are a great starting point for coaching around Career Transition issues. These questions are designed around basic coaching: clarifying, creating a vision, defining choice, identifying blocks and barriers, evaluating, prioritizing, probing, and scaling. Use these questions as touch-stones throughout the process. Categorized based on your client's specific needs and situation, these questions increase the scope of the coaching relationship.

Career Transition Wheel: The Career Transition Wheel is a self-awareness assessment you can use for yourself or your client to rate the level of satisfaction in each area of Career Transition. You or your client may want to broaden the scope of coaching to encompass each area and create the ideal career.

Wheel Specific Questions: As your coaching partnership deepens and gaps in career transition skills present themselves, you can target different areas of Career Transition more in-depth through these questions. These can even prolong the coaching partnership and develop more awareness around Career Transition.

Career Values / Qualities Assessment: Rating Career Transition Values by how important they are to you and how much you walk your talk can help you identify where gaps may be in Career Transition Skills. This is an excellent resource in identifying areas and opportunities for growth.

Blank Wheel: Using the Blank Wheel, you can fill in your or your client's top 8 Career Transition Values / Qualities and rank these to fill the gaps of creating their ideal Career Transition. You can also develop new coaching assignments and opportunities around each area.

Career Transition Quotes: This collection of Career Transition Quotes is a great resource for either your own marketing efforts or to deepen the level of thinking for your clients. Use these quotes to send inspirational emails, add to your website, use as topics for your newsletters or to Tweet.

SMART Goals Checklist: SMART Goals help ensure success. Goals that are unattainable or unreasonable are a direct line to failure. Failure stifles excitement, passion, and commitment. To ensure the success of your clients, check each goal against the SMART Goals checklist to determine the viability of the goal.

Additional Uses for This Book

Coaching / Consulting Role

→ Use the Wheel Assessment in a Complementary Session

→ Assess a client's level of satisfaction in the 8 key areas of the Career Transition Wheel

→ Use SMART Goals checklist as an evaluation & progression tool

→ Identify strengths & gaps in each area of the Career Transition Wheel in an introductory session to establish the foundation

→ Create accountability around the SMART Goals checklist

→ Identify strengths & gaps in each area of the Career Transition Wheel

→ Identify initial coaching goals

→ Use the questions as preparation for coaching sessions

→ Create customized assignments using the questions

→ Create visualizations & meditations based around the Career Transition Wheel segments or Questions

→ Use quotes in sessions to stimulate fresh perspectives

→ Add quotes to client emails for inspiration

→ Create a customized assignment by journaling on quotes

→ Create a mastermind or group discussion around a specific quote

→ Help clients set goals using the SMART Goals checklist

Product & Services Development

→ Use this book and the Career Transition Wheel as your Signature Program

→ Use Wheel Assessment in a workshop as an assessment or discussion tool

→ Add the Career Transition Wheel Assessment to your current Signature Program product

→ Use questions as an idea generator

→ Create an E-course / E-book / E-workbook series around segments of the Career Transition Wheel

→ Develop workshops & seminars around segments of the Wheel

→ Form Mastermind Groups around key Career Transition Wheel segments

→ Use the Career Transition Values / Qualities list as an idea generator

→ Write an E-course / E-book / E-workbook on a grouping of the Career Transition Values

→ Create Workshops & Seminars on a grouping of Career Transition Values

→ Add a quote to a product or presentation for inspiration or point emphasis

→ Use quote in workshop as a discussion topic

→ Use SMART Goals checklist in a workshop as tool to move participants forward

Marketing / Business Development

→ Use the Career Transition Wheel Assessment as a prospect pre-qualifier

→ Create a prequalifying survey for prospects with questions

→ Use questions or quotes in ezine / newsletter

→ Post a question / quote to your target audience on a LinkedIn Discussion

→ Use a series of questions to outline a promotional teleclass

→ Create a free download of questions around a particular topic

→ Use questions in Blog & Twitter Posts

→ Write an article based on the questions

→ Write an article based on an individual Career Transition Value

→ Use the Career Transition Values assessment as a pre-coaching prep form

→ Create an ezine / newsletter around individual Career Transition Value

→ Post a quote on your blog / Facebook / LinkedIn asking for comments about how it relates to the topic

→ Use a quote to inspire a podcast or video

→ Use quote to motivate article idea

→ Post Quote on Blog / Twitter

Open-Ended vs. Closed-Ended Questions

Open-Ended questions invite others to discuss in detail what is important to them. They are used to gather information, establish rapport, and increase understanding. These questions do not lead and are not geared towards expected outcomes. When used, the asker must be willing to listen and respond appropriately.

Closed-Ended questions are used to elicit a definitive answer. Use only when you want a definite yes or no. They are particularly useful when gaining a commitment.

Ask Open-Ended questions whenever possible.

Open-Ended Questions Start with:	Closed-Ended Questions Start with:
Who	Is
What	Does
How	Are
Why	Do
When	Will
Where	Can

General Career Transition Questions

Clarifying

Clarifying questions are designed to lay the groundwork and foundation for attaining goals. They set the stage, remove ambiguity, elicit details, and supply known facts.

Ask Clarifying Questions when you need a clear picture of where the questionee is currently at, what resources are available, what perspectives they have, as well as want a picture of what at and where the questionee is coming from, what they want, and what is the reality of the situation.

Ask these questions as a starting point, to establish a framework.

Example of Clarifying Questions

Questionee: I want to feel more freedom in my life.

Questioner: What do you mean by 'more freedom'?

Questionee: I mean to have the ability to do what I want when I want to.

Questioner: Give me an example.

Clarifying Questions

→ Who has the kind of career you seek?

→ Who supports you?

→ Who would you be if you stayed where you are?

→ Who has made an impact on your career so far?

→ Who inspires you to achieve your dreams?

→ What career(s) would you absolutely never want to do? Why?

→ What career(s) are you considering?

→ What makes a good job great?

→ What are your key reasons for changing careers?

→ What careers intrigue you most?

→ If you had no career, what would happen?

→ What decision is yours alone to make?

→ What would happen if you never made that decision?

→ Where have you done your best work?

→ Where do you want to go?

→ Where could your skills and talents best be used?

→ Where have you had the most success so far?

→ Where is the world looking for someone like you?

→ Where would you most like to work?

→ When has your career failed in the past?

→ When has it succeeded?

→ When was the first time you thought about making this change?

→ When might you begin to make this transition?

→ Why did that career / job end?

→ Why do you want to change careers?

→ Why not do what you have always done?

→ Why change?

→ Why has finding a new career become so critical?

→ How do you typically deal with change?

→ How certain are you that you need to change careers?

→ How much do you need to earn?

→ How do you define career?

Visioning

Visioning questions are designed to establish a desired end result. These questions create a picture of the future so a plan on how to get there can be created.

Visioning Questions allow the questionee to "see" the result they are working to achieve. This opens possibilities, engages creativity, and keeps motivation high and direction clear.

Ask Visioning Questions when creating a new reality, establishing an end-result, identifying the ideal, or giving direction to move forward.

Example of Visioning Questions

Questioner: What would you ideally like to see happen?

Questionee: I would like to move to the country away from the noise and congestion of the city. I would like to grow my own food, and living more simply. I would like to see the stars at night and hear the crickets sing.

Questioner: In this ideal vision, what do you see yourself doing?

Questionee: I see myself writing that book I keep talking about and having time to putter around in my flower garden.

Questioner: How would you feel?

Questionee: I see myself really happy, living a good life with the people I love, enjoying the things that give my life meaning.

Questioner: That is a beautiful picture for you.

Questionee: Yes it is!

Visioning Questions

→ Who would you like to be?

→ Who would you be if you had an ideal career?

→ Who are you without your ideal career?

→ What would be an ideal career for you?

→ What would your life look like if you loved your work?

→ What would you most like to do?

→ What would be your dream career?

→ What industry are you most interested in?

→ What field are you most interested in?

→ Where do you see yourself going?

→ Where would you like to be in 3 mo., 6 mo., a year from now?

→ Where would you most like to share your talents and abilities?

→ Where would the world benefit most from your gifts?

→ When you have the type of career you want, what will be different?

→ When is the best time to initiate this change?

→ When do you imagine you will have the career you desire?

→ When will you be ready to make this change?

→ Why do you want to make this change?

→ Why is it not the time to make this change?

→ Why do you imagine this change will make your life better?

→ Why is realizing your dream important?

→ How would having an ideal career change your life?

→ How often do you dream of a more satisfying career?

→ How can you use your skills / strengths to help you achieve your dream?

→ How would your life be different if you were truly happy in your career?

Choice

Choice Questions are meant to show options, empower, and accept responsibility. These questions lend to out of the box thinking and demonstrate options and opportunities.

Ask Choice Questions when questionee feels trapped, hopeless, or feels as though there is no other answer and needs a new perspective & empowering to move forward.

Example of Choice Question

Questionee: I don't know what to do. I really would like to attend that seminar next Saturday and Sunday but my husband wants to take the kids to the cabin that same weekend. We always do everything together.

Questioner: If you knew no-one would be upset, what options do you have to resolve this?

Questionee: You mean, if I went to the seminar and my husband took the boys to the cabin without me?

Questioner: What would happen if that could be the reality?

Questionee: Well that certainly would be different. Maybe that would work. I will talk with my husband tonight.

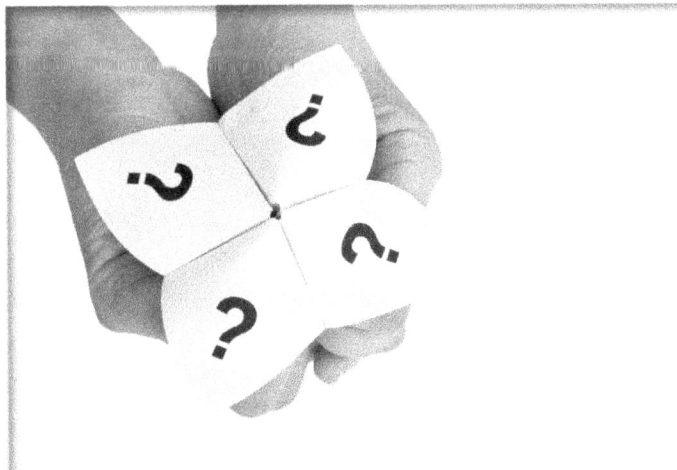

Choice Questions

→ Who would you be if you stayed where you are?

→ Who can you align with to help you achieve your dream?

→ Who can you reach out to for support?

→ From whom have you avoided getting help?

→ Who has supported your career choices in the past?

→ Who has criticized your career choices in the past?

→ Who supports this decision?

→ Whose decision is that ultimately?

→ What does your career require of you?

→ What is yours, and yours alone, to do?

→ What do you really want to do?

→ What difference would you like to make?

→ What is your number one decision to make?

→ What are your choices here?

→ What have you avoided making a decision on?

→ What one decision is waiting for you to make?

→ Where would you like to live?

→ Where would you like to work?

→ Where would you like to travel?

→ Where would that decision take you?

→ Where could that decision take you?

→ When do you need to make that decision?

→ When should this decision be made?

→ When would you like to do that?

→ When do you plan to begin?

→ When has making clear decisions regarding your career been hardest?

→ Why decide now?

→ Why is now not the time to decide?

→ Why that particular choice?

→ Why is making a decision crucial?

→ Why would you not take that option?

→ Why are you hesitating with this decision?

→ Why have you decided that?

→ Why did you choose that direction?

→ How often do you make clear decisions?

→ How would that choice help you?

→ How would that choice hurt you?

→ How often do you avoid making decisions regarding your dreams?

→ How could this choice help you move forward?

→ How critical is this choice to achieving your goal?

→ How would you like to proceed?

Blocks & Barriers

These questions are designed to uncover & examine, what is stopping the questionee from moving forward, seeing progress, and gaining what they truly want.

Ask Blocks and Barrier Questions when you sense hesitation, resistance, goal hopping, or a belief they are unable to move forward.

Example of Blocks & Barriers Questions

Questionee: I really would like to date again but can't seem to put myself out there.

Questioner: What do you think is getting in the way?

Questionee: I'm not sure.....maybe my fear.

Questioner: Fear of what?

Questionee: Fear of not being attractive enough....of no one being interested in me.

Questioner: So you would rather stay home alone where it is safe than risk getting rejected again.

Questionee: As pitiful as that sounds, yes, I think that is it.

Questioner: How well will that work for you?

Questionee: Not very well at all since I want to meet someone! I guess we have some more work to do!

Questioner: I guess we do!

Blocks & Barriers Questions

→ Who in your life has been a dream-dasher?

→ Who has criticized your choice of careers in the past?

→ Who might try to stop you moving forward?

→ Who would you become if nothing got in your way?

→ Who disapproves of your chosen path?

→ Who are you trying to please?

→ To whom do you ultimately answer?

→ Who supports your dreams?

→ Who doubts you will ever do this?

→ Who taught you to limit yourself?

→ What blocks are holding you back?

→ What false notions about yourself have to go in order to embrace this change?

→ What would you say to your dream-dashers now?

→ What might get in your way from moving into this career?

→ What is holding you back from embracing your true gifts?

→ What is your biggest challenge today?

→ What makes that challenge particularly difficult?

→ What are you waiting for?

→ What haven't you considered doing because of fear?

→ What courageous step can you take today?

→ What might prevent you from moving forward?

→ Where do you limit yourself?

→ Where do you set yourself free?

→ Where are you absolutely sure of yourself?

→ Where are you in the dark?

→ Where are you stuck?

→ Where are you blind to your abilities?

→ Where are you deaf to your purpose?

→ Where are you numb to your true calling?

→ When have you felt the most off track in your career?

→ When have you felt the most spot on?

→ When are you going to move through that?

→ When have you stopped yourself in the past?

→ When might you stop yourself in the future?

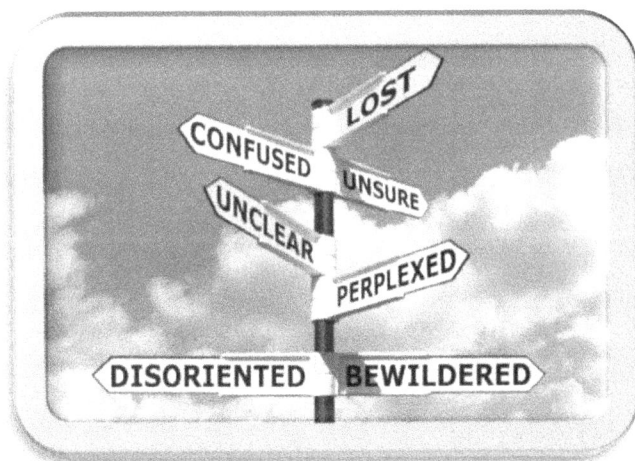

→ Why have you struggled with defining your career options?

→ Why aré you uncertain of your career at this point?

→ Why has this dream gone unfulfilled?

→ Why would you let that stop you?

→ Why not do it?

→ Why not move beyond that?

→ Why is this particular block so troubling for you?

→ Why is feeling career-less so debilitating?

→ Why wouldn't you give yourself every chance to succeed?

→ Why are you in a fog about which way to go?

→ How has your confusion about your career affected your relationships?

→ How often do you feel lost?

→ How could you continue without knowing your true path?

→ How can you get beyond that?

→ If that barrier was a living breathing thing, how would you describe it?

→ How can you get around it?

→ How can you go through it?

→ How can you rise up and move beyond?

Evaluating

Evaluating Questions determine criteria. They evaluate or estimate the nature, quality, extent or significance of situations. They assess factors such as needs, issues, processes, performance, and outcomes. They can also determine the cons of a situation.

Ask Evaluating Questions when the questionee needs to establish a clearer sense of their wants and needs related to a particular situation.

Example of Evaluating Questions

Questionee: I want to achieve more success at work.

Questioner: What would that look like?

Questionee: I would work more efficiently and get things done on time.

Questioner: What would be different if you were more efficient?

Questionee: I would lead meetings with more confidence and get more buy-in from the team.

Questioner: How would it feel if you achieved all of that?

Questionee: Great!

Evaluating Questions

→ Who do you most need support from to make this change?

→ Who could you talk to about that?

→ Who impacts you the most?

→ Who are you when you are at your best?

→ Who are you the most open with about your true aspirations? Why?

→ Who are you the least open with about your true aspirations? Why?

→ Who offers you the most support?

→ Who attempts to dash your dreams the most fervently?

→ Who believes in your dream with the greatest enthusiasm?

→ What would you change about your current job?

→ What was the worst thing about your career path?

→ If you had to describe your ideal career in just three words, what would they be?

→ What is your biggest career challenge today?

→ What makes that challenge particularly difficult?

→ What is the difference between a job and a career?

→ What is the difference between a career and a calling?

→ What are you waiting for?

→ What have you learned about pursuing this particular career?

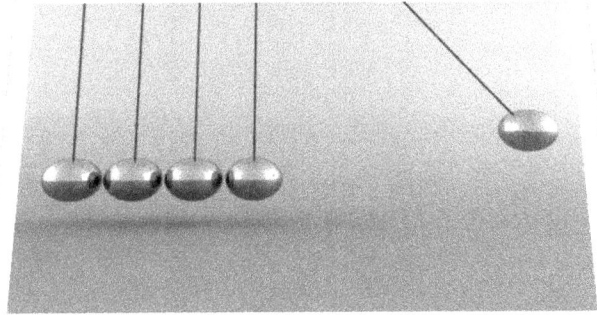

→ What are the key reasons you are questioning your career path?

→ What intrigues you most?

→ What type of people do you gravitate to?

→ What type of organizations interest you?

→ What would suit you best?

→ Where have your efforts been most appreciated?

→ Where have they been the least appreciated?

→ Where is the best place to go to gain the information you need?

→ Where would you most like to see yourself go?

→ Where could you be more focused in your career?

→ Where could you use more support?

→ Where can you use your skills to make the biggest difference?

→ When should someone leave a job?

→ When should someone stay?

→ When would having a career be irrelevant?

→ When would it be critical?

→ When are you most engaged with work?

→ When are you the least engaged with work?

→ When would having a career be irrelevant to ones calling?

→ When would it be critical?

→ When is the best time to pursue that?

→ Why is that important to you?

→ Why do people need a clear career path?

→ Why do you need a clear sense of direction?

→ Why is this change so important?

→ Why are you willing to take this up?

→ How eager are you to discover your true path?

→ How well do you navigate big changes?

→ How comfortable are you moving into a new career?

→ How does your need to earn a living affect your career choices?

→ How do you measure success in life?

→ How will you know you have found your true purpose?

→ How important is meaningful work to you?

→ Without them saying a word, how can to tell someone is satisfied with their chosen career?

Goal Setting

Goal Setting Questions are designed to move into and forward the action. They include aspects of accountability, step-by-step action, and an understanding of what needs to be done in order to accomplish the desired goal(s).

Goal Setting Questions are intended to set the questionee up for success. In order to accomplish his there are certain factors to be considered when designing a goal plan.

SMART Goals help construct a format for creating successful goals.

Ask Goal Setting Questions when the questionee is ready to move into action.

Example of Goal Setting Questions

Questionee: I decided I want to return to college and finish my degree.

Questioner: That's great! When would you like to begin?

Questionee: Next semester but I have some things I need to do first.

Questioner: What do you see as the 1st step to take to get started?

Questionee: Well, I need to talk with an admissions counselor and figure out what credits will transfer and how many credits I need to complete my degree. Then I have to decide which classes to start with.

Questioner: That sounds like a plan. When will you make the appointment?

Questionee: This week. I am excited!
(Move onto creating SMART Goals *pg71)

Goal Setting Questions

→ Who can help you do that?

→ Who else supports that?

→ Who might get in the way?

→ Who would you like to include in your plans?

→ Who needs this to happen?

→ What might get in your way of you achieving this?

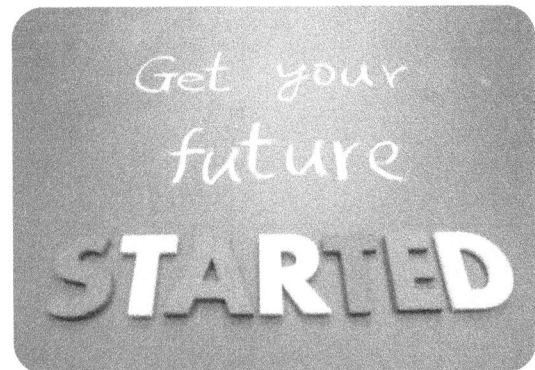

→ What do you need to succeed?

→ What motivates you to make this change?

→ What courageous step can you take today?

→ What would it take to achieve these goals?

→ What do you need to succeed with that?

→ What is the first thing you need to do?

→ What are the top 3-5 must-haves?

→ Where can you find the information you need?

→ Where do you imagine this goal will take you?

→ Where could you apply goal setting to achieve your dream?

→ When would you like to land a new position?

→ When would it be too late?

→ When do you want to accomplish this?

→ When do you want to begin?

→ When have you set goals before and not followed through?

→ When would you know you have succeeded?

→ When could you achieve this?

→ When are you going to begin?

→ When will you complete this?

→ Why is reaching that goal important to you?

→ Why is that goal necessary?

→ Why would you stop yourself from achieving that goal?

→ Why set that particular goal?

→ Why not set that goal?

→ How much energy do you have for this transition?

→ How quickly would you like to make this change?

→ How do you inspire & motivate yourself to move forward?

→ How would you know you have not succeeded?

→ How would you know you have reached your goal?

→ How would your life change if those goals were achieved?

Prioritizing

Prioritizing Questions identifies and weighs importance, values and benefits. They can also be used to rank & order.

Prioritizing Questions are great to use in conjunction with Goal Setting Questions and can also help reduce overwhelm.

Ask Prioritizing Questions when the questionee needs to put their priorities in order or examine what is important to them.

Example of Prioritizing Questions:

Questionee: I have so many things I need to get done. I feel overwhelmed!

Questioner: That is understandable considering all you have on your plate. Let's make a list of everything you have to do.

Questionee: OK.

(Together they create a list of to-do's)

Questionee: That's a lot! No wonder I feel overwhelmed.

Questioner: I hear you! Let's chunk it down. Of these 12 items, which are the most urgent and necessary to get done this week?

Questionee: I would have to say numbers 3, 6 and 7. The others can wait. I feel much better.

Prioritizing Questions

→ With whom do you most want to work?

→ Who would you most like to become part of your inner circle?

→ Who would you become if that was your top priority?

→ Who is your top priority?

→ Who do you need to make more of a priority?

→ Who is the lowest person on your priority list?

→ What type of organizations do you gravitate to?

→ What type of organizations would you never want to work for?

→ What are the top 3-5 must-haves for your next job?

→ What would you most like to get out of your career?

→ What is more important when choosing a career, the head or the heart?

→ If your head alone made the decision, what career would you choose?

→ If your heart alone made the decision, what career would you choose?

→ What would a combination of the two look like?

→ What place should intuition have when deciding?

→ What career would suit you best?

→ What would you most like to get out of your career?

→ What would you most like life to give you?

→   What would you most like to give?

→   What are your greatest needs right now?

→   What are your top 3 must-haves going forward?

→   What are the top 3 things your career wants from you?

→   If you could only have one career, what would that be?

→   What can / can't you do without?

→   What is your number one priority?

→   Where do you need to set clearer priorities?

→   Where are your current priorities taking you?

→   Where do you want your priorities to take you?

→   When can you make that a priority?

→   When do you need that on the top of your list?

→   When does your career influence your priorities?

→   When do your current priorities impact your career path?

→   Why do you need to make that a priority?

→   Why is that important to you?

→   Why not make that the most important thing in your life?

→   Why are you keeping that on the bottom of your list?

→   In the grand scheme of things, how important is having a satisfying career really?

→   How willing are you to take that risk?

→   How could shifting your priorities help you stay true to your path?

urgent

Probing

Probing Questions make the questionee go deeper, drawing out more details, concerns, challenges, knowledge, and issues about a particular situation. A good Probing Question requires thought. These questions are used to get out the root of the situation, and reveal thoughts, feelings, and details under the surface.

Ask Probing Questions when going deeper into an issue or concern will bring greater insight and help uncover new awareness; thoughts and feelings lying below the surface.

Example of Probing Questions

Questionee: I really don't want to do my presentation tomorrow.

Questioner: Why not?

Questionee: I don't know. Even though I put a lot of time into preparing it, I guess I don't think it's very good. I'd rather hold off until I can make it better.

Questioner: From what you described last time, it appears you have a solid presentation.

Questionee: Yeah, I guess so. I just think it could be better.

Questioner: Putting the presentation itself aside, what are you really worried about?

Questionee: (Pause) That I will freeze...nothing will come out of my mouth and look like a bumbling fool!

Questioner: That is quite a worry.

Questionee: I didn't realize how anxious I am about speaking to the group.

Questioner: How would it be for us to work on that together?

Questionee: Yes, please! It would be great.

Probing Questions

→   Who has the kind of career you admire?

→   Who inspires you to achieve your dreams?

→   Who do you most need support from to make this change?

→   Who in the past tampered with your dreams?

→   Who in the past supported your dreams?

→   Who has most influenced your ideas?

→   With whom do you talk about your aspirations?

→   What type of career would make your heart sing?

→   What makes you believe you deserve a more satisfying career?

→   What would you do if you knew you could not fail?

→   What have you always wanted to try doing, but never thought you could?

→   What qualities and characteristics would make up an ideal career for you?

→   What have you thought about doing?

→   What is the hardest thing about not knowing what direction to take?

→   What is driving you to make this change?

→   What beliefs do you have about your career so far?

→   What do you really want to do?

→   What haven't you tried yet that just might bring you joy?

→ What is the hardest thing about being in transition?

→ What type of career would bring out your best?

→ If you were in your advanced years and had an opportunity to tell a fresh-out-of-college young adult the most important thing you learned about building a career, what you tell them?

→ What difference would you like to make?

→ Where can you use your skills to make the biggest difference?

→ Where would you like to serve?

→ Where would you like to lead?

→ Where has your career gone underground?

→ Where has your career soared?

→ Where does your career path want to take you?

→ Where do you want to take your career?

→ When are you at your very best?

→ When have you been absolutely sure that this is the career for you?

→ When will you know you have landed in the right career?

→ When will you give yourself every opportunity to realize this dream?

→ Why would that make a difference?

→ Why is having a satisfying career important?

→ Why are you willing to make this change?

→ Why is discovering your right livelihood an urgent matter?

→ Why not do what you have always done?

→ Why is the risk worth it?

→ Why has finding your true vocation become so critical?

→ How do you share your gifts?

→ How much do your thoughts affect your career choices?

→ How important is meaningful work to you?

→ How do you know when a career falls short?

→ How do you know when it excels?

→ In the grand scheme of things, how important is a career really?

→ How will you know you have found your true vocation?

→ How will this career change you?

→ How would someone know you were living the life of your dreams?

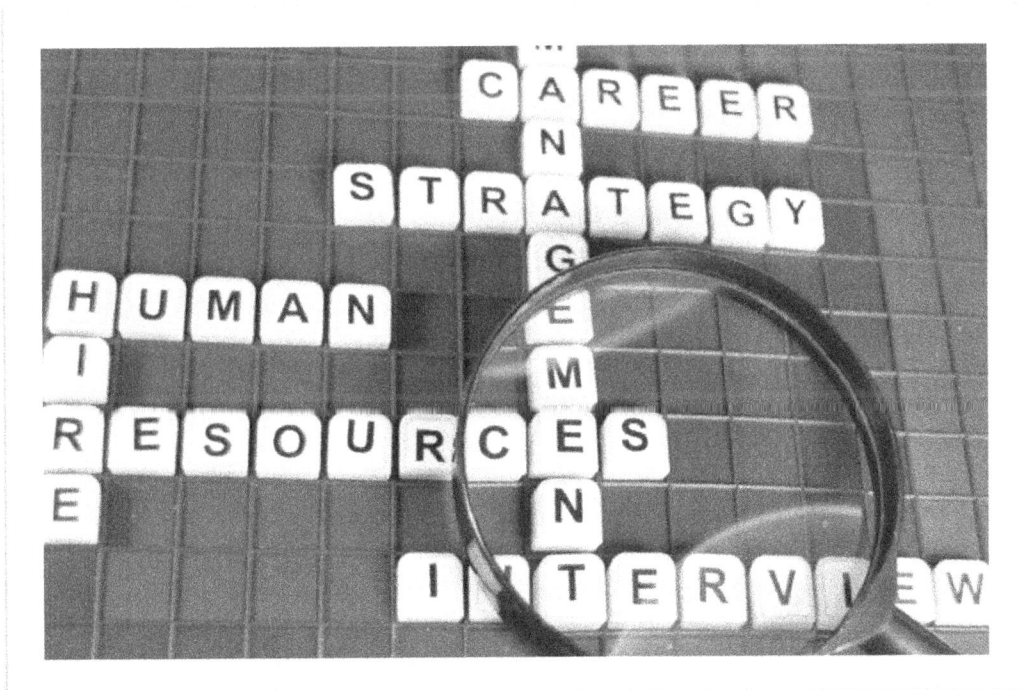

New Perspectives

New Perspective Questions are designed to shift the direction of thinking. By shifting thinking the questionee can shift the way they approach the world and situations. These questions often create "aha" moments as they elicit options and possibilities previously not considered.

Ask New Perspective Questions when the questionee persists in levels of thinking that include anger, blame, victim, trapped or when they are unable / unwilling to see alternatives.

Example of New Perspective Questions

Questionee: I think my sister is upset with me.

Questioner: What makes you think that?

Questionee: Because she hasn't returned my calls this week.

Questioner: How certain are you she is upset with you?

Questionee: Well, why else wouldn't she call me back?

Questioner: Great question! What might be some other reasons she hasn't called you back yet?

Questionee: Well, maybe she's really busy with work. I know she had a big project she was working on and her boss can set some tough deadlines. I bet that's it.

New Perspective Questions

→ Who could you talk to about your aspirations?

→ Who could give you a fresh perspective?

→ Who are you becoming?

→ Who would you be if everything lined up perfectly?

→ Who can you become?

→ If money wasn't an issue, what would you love to do?

→ What haven't you tried that would bring you joy?

→ What haven't you considered because of fear?

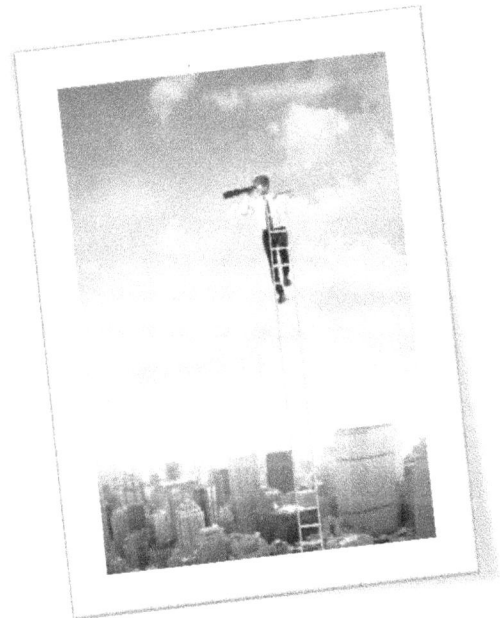

→ What might be a new way of looking at that?

→ What might be a different way to think about that?

→ What feeling would you like to experience?

→ Where haven't you looked for the answers yet?

→ Where will you be once you land in your perfect career?

→ Where could this new career path take you?

→ Where are you less than eager to make this change?

→ Where are you chomping at the bit to get going already?

→ Where would you end up if nothing changes?

→ Where would you like to breathe life into your dream?

→ When is a career a straight line?

→ When is it a curve?

→ When will your true vocation be revealed?

→ When does one's passion and work line up?

→ When could you take hold of that?

→ When will your life be just perfect?

→ When have you been the most excited about a new career?

→ Why risk it?

→ Why does it matter?

→ Why isn't your current career working for you?

→ Why put yourself through this?

→ Why do you feel you need a change of careers?

→ How would taking that risk serve you?

→ How do you measure success in a career?

→ How do you define success?

→ Without them saying a word, how can to tell someone is satisfied with their career?

→ How would uncovering your true vocation change your life?

→ How would uncovering your true vocation change the life of others?

→ How can you discover what is yours to do?

→ How would you benefit the most from finding your true work?

→ How would others benefit?

Scaling

Scaling Questions help gauge and determine the level of concern, commitment, and importance. They are a tool that identifies where the questionee would position themselves, the situation or determining a level. Scaling Questions can be used to help measure progress, attitude and behavioral change, and situational shifts.

Ask Scaling Questions when the questionee wants to gauge the level of concern, commitment, or importance of a situation or concern.

Example of Scaling Questions

Questioner: On a scale of 1-10, 1 being not at all and 10 being extremely, how important is that for you?

Questionee: I would say about an 8.5.

Questioner: That's pretty important!

Questionee: Yes, it really it.

Scaling Questions

→ On a Scale of 1 to 10 (10 = completely satisfied and 1 = completely dissatisfied) where would you rank yourself with your current line of work? Why did you rank yourself that way?

→ On a Scale of 1 to 10 (10 = absolutely confident and 1 = not confident at all) how confident are you that you will achieve your ideal career? Why did you rank yourself that way?

→ On a Scale of 1 to 10 (10 = completely and 1 = not at all) how comfortable are you making this career change? Why did you rank yourself that way?

→ On a Scale of 1 to 10 (10 = extremely important and 1 = not important at all) how important is it for you to be happy at work? Why did you rank yourself that way?

→ On a Scale of 1 to 10 (10 = absolutely and 1 = not at all) how happy are you with your work life as it is? Why did you rank yourself that way?

→ On a Scale of 1 to 10 (10 = all the time and 1 = never) how often do you doubt your dream? Why did you rank yourself that way?

→ On a Scale of 1 to 10 (10 = completely and 1 = not at all) how fully are you using your skills and talents? Why did you rank yourself that way?

→ On a Scale of 1 to 10 (10 = extremely and 1 = not at all) how optimistic are you about your future? Why did you rank yourself that way?

→ On a Scale of 1 to 10 (10 = extremely and 1 = not at all) how passionate are you about your true calling? Why did you rank yourself that way?

→ On a Scale of 1 to 10 (10 = completely and 1 = not at all) how eager are you to begin? Why did you rank yourself that way?

Career Transition Wheel

Directions: for each section of the Career Transition Wheel, circle the number that represents your current level of satisfaction in that area. The higher the number, the greater your level of satisfaction.

CAREER TRANSITION

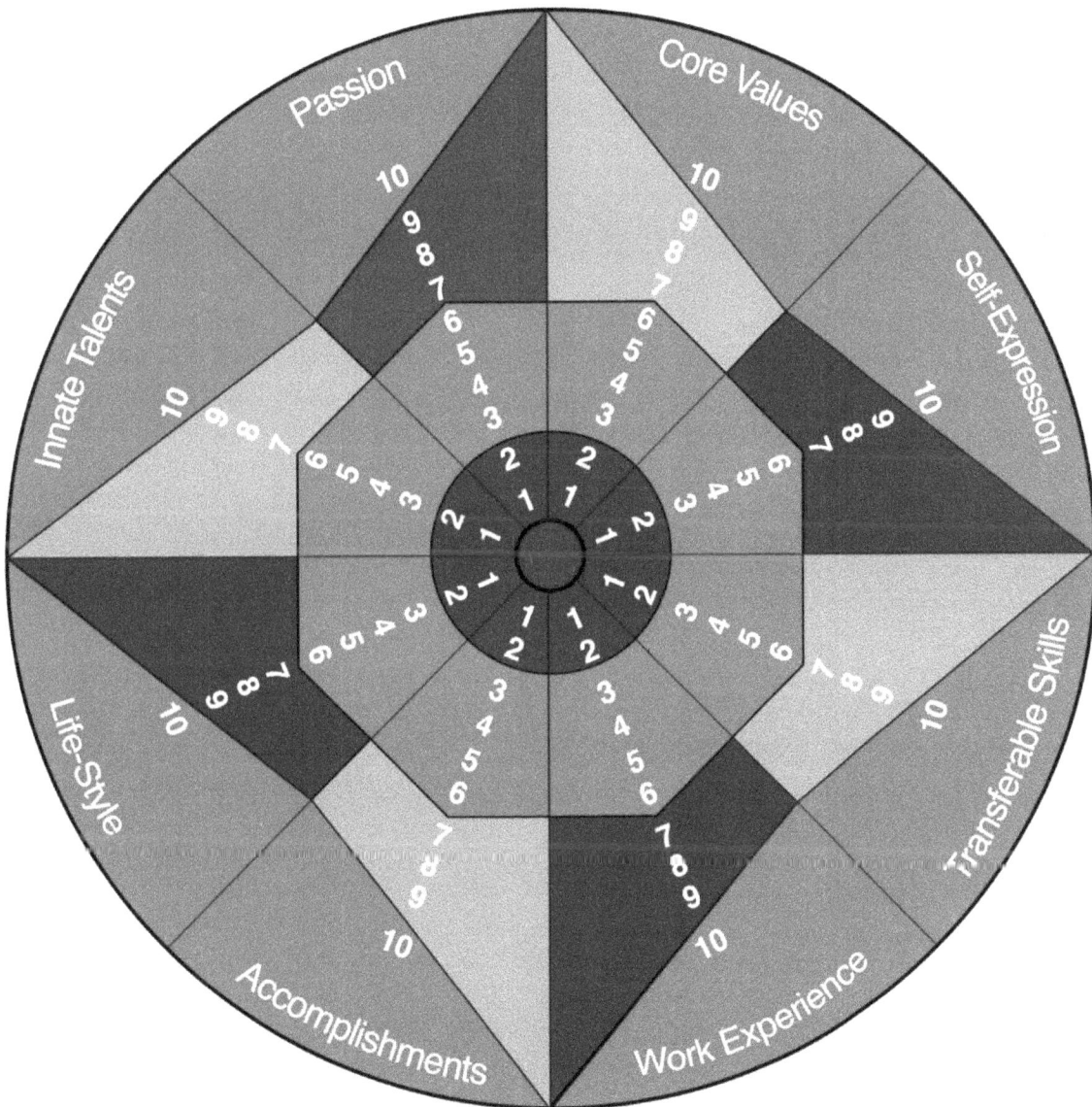

Passion

Who

→ Who would you be without passion?

→ Who exemplifies passion for you?

→ With whom do you have the most difficult time being passionate? Why?

→ With whom do you have the easiest time being passionate? Why?

→ Who would you be if passion fueled your life and / or work?

What

→ What does having passion for your work mean to you?

→ What are the benefits of being passionate?

→ What is the downside?

→ What three qualities epitomize passion?

→ What could you do to become more passionate in your career / work?

Where

→ Where do you need to be more passionate?

→ Where does your passion want to take you?

→ Where has passion been missing from your career / work?

→ Where is your passion the weakest?

→ Where is your passion the strongest?

When

→ When is passion most essential?

→ When is passion a liability?

→ When would be the best time to engage your passion?

→ When are you the most passionate?

→ When are you the least?

Why

→ Why is passion necessary in a career?

→ Why is passion important for an organization?

→ Why don't you feel passion for that anymore?

→ Why would having passion for your work be important?

→ Why would you take a job you are not passionate about?

How

→ How passionate are you about your career?

→ How passionate would you like to be?

→ How will you begin to reclaim your passion for your work?

→ How can passion be cultivated?

→ How would others benefit from your passion?

Your Questions on Passion

→ _____

→ _____

→ _____

→ _____

→ _____

Innate Talents

Who

→ Who supported your talents as a child? In what way?

→ Who supports your talents now? How?

→ Who tries to squelch your talents?

→ Who has benefited the most from your talents?

→ Who would you be if your innate talents came fully alive?

What

→ What is talent?

→ What are your innate talents?

→ What type of career / job would best support your talents?

→ What talents have you consistently used in your work-life?

→ What talents have gone underground?

Where

→ Where have your talents been used the most?

→ Where have they been used the least?

→ Where is your talent comfort zone?

→ Where do you need to use your innate talents more? Why?

→ Where do you see your talent taking you?

When

→ When do you find your talents most engaged?

→ When do you find them least engaged?

→ When will the world see your talents expressed in all their glory?

→ When in your career have your talents been most utilized?

→ When have then been used the least?

Why

→ Why would using your innate talents help your career?

→ Why aren't you using your talents to their fullest?

→ Why do you like using your talents?

→ Why would you take a job that squashes your talents?

→ Why is talent essential in any career?

How

→ How do your innate talents show up at work?

→ How would you most like to use your talents?

→ How were your innate talents expressed as a child?

→ How have you suppressed your talents?

→ How would others benefit from your talents?

Your Questions on Innate Talent

→ _____

→ _____

→ _____

→ _____

→ _____

Transferable Skills

Who

→ Who has benefited the most from your skills and abilities in the past?

→ Who could benefit most from your skills and abilities now?

→ Who defines what skills are most important?

→ Who can help you develop your skills?

→ Who inspired you to gain the skills you have? In what way?

What

→ What are your transferable skills?

→ What are your primary skills?

→ What skills would be the most important to carry with you into your next career?

→ What are your secondary skills?

→ What skills would help you most with this transition?

Where

→ Where do you see your skills being best used?

→ Where could these skills take you?

→ Where are your skills the strongest?

→ Where are they the weakest?

→ Where have your skills made the most impact?

When

→ When do you use your skills the most effectively?

→ When do you find your skills least used?

→ When have you felt the most skilled?

→ When have you felt the least skilled?

→ When would you like to develop that skill?

Why

→ Why do you feel your skills are transferable?

→ Why would those particular skills be helpful in your new career?

→ Why have you cultivated those skills?

→ Why are having these skills important?

→ Why not take those skills with you?

How

→ How can you use those skills in your next career?

→ How would you describe your skills to a potential employer?

→ How can you utilize your skills to achieve your goals?

→ How can you strengthen your skills for better results?

→ How would you best like to use your skills?

Your Questions on Transferable Skills

→ _____

→ _____

→ _____

→ _____

→ _____

Work Experience

Who

→ With whom did you most enjoy working?

→ Who helped you succeed in your former role?

→ Who could you use as a reference?

→ If you could, who would you most like to work for again? Why?

→ From whom did you learn the most?

What

→ What work experience seems the most relevant now?

→ What in your background are you the proudest of?

→ What strengths and gaps do you see in your background?

→ What part of your background / experience do you most want to highlight?

→ What was your all-time best work experience?

Where

→ Where have you been the most satisfied in a career / job? Why?

→ Where have you been the least satisfied? Why?

→ Where do you see your experience taking you now?

→ Where would you like to gain new work experience?

→ Where did you enjoy working most / least?

When

→ When were you the happiest at work? Why?

→ When did you struggle most? Why?

→ When has your background / experience come in handy? Why?

→ When was your work the most satisfying? Why?

→ When did you feel the most respected for your knowledge?

Why

→ Why is your work experience important?

→ Why are you considering a career transition at this time?

→ Why have you been dissatisfied with past positions?

→ Why would you benefit from new experiences?

→ Why is making this decision so difficult?

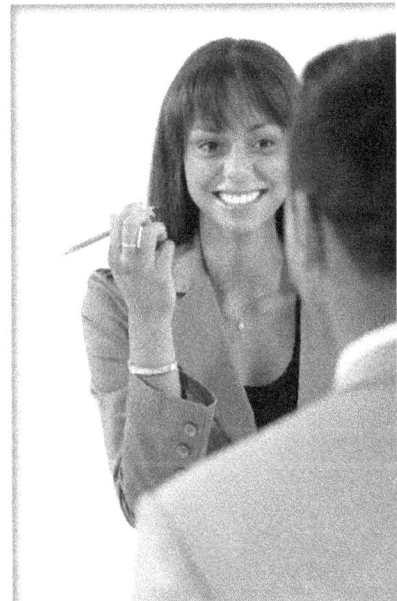

How

→ How does your work experience relate to what you want to do now?

→ How can you leverage your past experience?

→ How would you describe your previous work experience in three words?

→ How relevant is your experience?

→ How can you make your experience work for you?

Your Questions on Work Experience

→ _____

→ _____

→ _____

→ _____

→ _____

Accomplishments

Who

→ Who helped you achieve that?

→ Who has tried to sabotage your success in the past?

→ Who has been your most ardent supporter?

→ Who would you have become if you had accomplished more?

→ Who in you, wants to be more and do more?

What

→ What is your greatest accomplishment?

→ What does this achievement say about you?

→ What beliefs do you hold about what you have accomplished?

→ What is left to achieve?

→ What type of achievement would mean the world to you?

Where

→ Where are your greatest career achievements?

→ Where have your accomplishments fallen short?

→ Where would you like to achieve more in your career?

→ Where do you feel the most accomplished?

→ Where do you feel the least accomplished?

When

→ When have you felt the most successful?

→ When have you felt the least successful?

→ When have your accomplishments been the most meaningful?

→ When would you like to achieve that?

→ When have your accomplishments been celebrated?

Why

→ Why are your accomplishments important?

→ Why have you been driven to succeed?

→ Why would you feel better if you had accomplished more?

→ Why was that particular achievement meaningful?

→ Why do you have a hard time acknowledging your accomplishments?

How

→ How do your achievements express the essence of who you are?

→ How would you feel if you had accomplished more?

→ How can your accomplishments help you now?

→ How did you achieve that?

→ How accomplished do you feel you are?

Your Questions on Accomplishments

→ _____

→ _____

→ _____

→ _____

Core Values

Who

→ Who honors your core values?

→ Who finds your core values questionable?

→ Who would you be without your core values?

→ Who would you become if you lived by your values every minute of every day?

→ Who holds the same values as you?

What

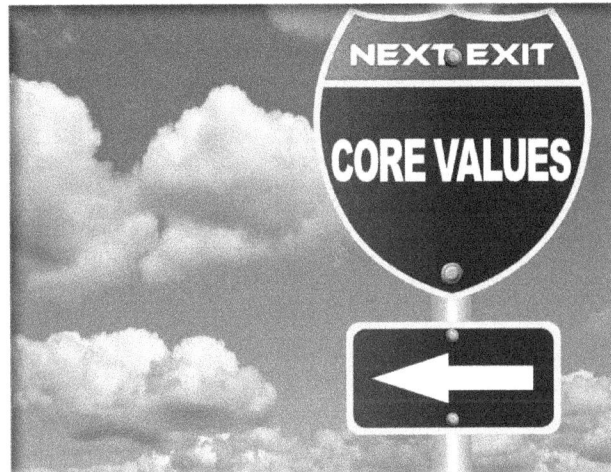

→ What are your core values?

→ What do your values say about you?

→ What career choice would best support your core values?

→ In your work, what values have been the hardest to express?

→ In your work, what values have been the easiest to express?

Where

→ Where in the past have your values been compromised?

→ Where do your values and career choices intersect?

→ Where would you be without your values?

→ Where could your values be stronger?

→ Where have you been the most aware of your values?

When

→ As a professional, when have you compromised your own values?

→ When do you most need to stand by your values?

→ When have your values saved you?

→ When are you going to embrace your values completely?

→ When could your values help you most during this transition?

Why

→ Why is working according to your values important?

→ Why have you sacrificed your values in the past?

→ Why doesn't that align with your core values?

→ Why is identifying your core values so important?

→ Why should your career be an expression of what you value?

How

→ How do your core values keep you focused on what's important?

→ How can your core values help you through this transition?

→ How often do you make decisions based on your values?

→ How would you like your career to reflect your values?

→ How can you find a career that aligns with your values?

Your Questions on Core Values

→ _____

→ _____

→ _____

→ _____

→ _____

Self-Expression

Who

→ Who encourages you to be who you are?

→ Who tries to silence your authentic self?

→ Who would you be if you had no fear?

→ Who are you?

→ Who, in you, wants to be given full voice?

What

→ What does self-expression mean to you?

→ What would work be like if you could be yourself 100% of the time?

→ What are you afraid to show?

→ What would help you overcome that fear?

→ If nothing held you back, what would you tell the world?

Where

→ Where have you been the most expressive? Why?

→ Where have you been the most withheld? Why?

→ Where would you like to be more expressive in your work?

→ Where have you been the most creative at work?

→ Where would you like to be more creative?

When

→ When are you most expressive?

→ When have you enjoyed your work the most? Why?

→ When do you need to be more expressive?

→ When do you need to let go of fear most?

→ When is the best time to tell the world who you are?

Why

→ Why is self-expression so important to you?

→ Why do you want to express yourself through your work?

→ Why is self-expression necessary?

→ Why have you held back in the past?

→ Why would that stop you from being who you are?

How

→ How comfortable are you expressing yourself at work?

→ How can you express yourself more?

→ How would your career benefit if you were more self-expressive?

→ How have you held yourself back?

→ How does your career support self-expression?

Your Questions on Self-Expression

→ _____

→ _____

→ _____

→ _____

→ _____

Lifestyle

Who

→ Who would be impacted most by your career change?

→ Who would you like to include in your inner circle?

→ Who is missing from your life?

→ Who helps you maintain your current lifestyle?

→ Who cares the most about what changes you make?

What

→ What lifestyle do you want your career to support?

→ What are you willing to let go of?

→ What career would give you the income you need / want?

→ In what way does your lifestyle work against you?

→ What would work-life balance look like for you?

Where

→ Where do you want to live?

→ Where could you see yourself moving?

→ Where do you get your sense of security?

→ Where are you feeling vulnerable?

→ Where might this career change take you?

When

→ When do you enjoy life most?

→ When do you enjoy life least?

→ When has your work / career impinged on your personal life?

→ When would you like to make that lifestyle change?

→ When has life been the sweetest?

Why

→ Why did you choose that lifestyle?

→ Why is having that amount of income important to you?

→ Why are those things important for you to have?

→ Why would you change your lifestyle?

→ Why not make that change?

How

→ How important is it to maintain this lifestyle?

→ How does maintaining this lifestyle serve you?

→ How could making some changes serve you better?

→ How might your lifestyle be impacted by this career change?

→ How could you determine what is most important to maintain?

Your Questions on Lifestyle

→ _____

→ _____

→ _____

→ _____

→ _____

Career Transition Values / Qualities Assessment

Directions: Identify your top 8 Career Transition Values / Qualities. How closely do you live these Values / Qualities?

☐	Accomplishment	☐	Customer Focused
☐	Achievement	☐	Dedication
☐	Acumen	☐	Discipline
☐	Adaptability	☐	Diversity
☐	Adventure	☐	Driven
☐	Ambition	☐	Education
☐	Analytical	☐	Endurance
☐	Aptitude	☐	Enthusiasm
☐	Artistic Expression	☐	Ethical
☐	Assertiveness	☐	Entrepreneurial
☐	Attainment	☐	Evocative
☐	Authenticity	☐	Excitement
☐	Background	☐	Experience
☐	Balance	☐	Expertise
☐	Beauty	☐	Fearless
☐	Being the Boss	☐	Financial Security
☐	Capacity	☐	Flexibility
☐	Change Agent	☐	Focused
☐	Commitment	☐	Forward Thinking
☐	Community Involvement	☐	Freedom
☐	Competency	☐	Fresh Start
☐	Connection	☐	Fulfillment
☐	Continual Learning	☐	Fun
☐	Contribution	☐	Growth
☐	Cooperative	☐	Healthy Lifestyle
☐	Courage	☐	Honesty
☐	Creativity	☐	Humility

- [ ] Humor
- [ ] Imagination
- [ ] Independence
- [ ] Industrious
- [ ] Innate Talent
- [ ] Innovative
- [ ] Inspirational
- [ ] Integration
- [ ] Integrity
- [ ] Intelligence
- [ ] Interest
- [ ] Interdependence
- [ ] Intuition
- [ ] Inventive
- [ ] Joy
- [ ] Leadership
- [ ] Life-Work Balance
- [ ] Living My Dream
- [ ] Loyalty
- [ ] Maturity
- [ ] Meaningful Work
- [ ] Motivational
- [ ] Objectivity
- [ ] Openness
- [ ] Opportunistic
- [ ] Optimistic
- [ ] Organize
- [ ] Partnership
- [ ] Passion
- [ ] Patience
- [ ] People-Focused
- [ ] Philanthropy

- [ ] Play
- [ ] Power
- [ ] Pro-Active
- [ ] Productive Purpose
- [ ] Recognition
- [ ] Respect Responsible
- [ ] Risk Taker
- [ ] Scientific
- [ ] Self-Care
- [ ] Self-Expression
- [ ] Service-Oriented
- [ ] Simplicity
- [ ] Skills & Abilities
- [ ] Spontaneity
- [ ] Structured
- [ ] Successful
- [ ] Supportive
- [ ] Synthesis
- [ ] Team Work
- [ ] Technical
- [ ] Thought Leader
- [ ] Tolerance
- [ ] Unstructured
- [ ] Visionary
- [ ] Wisdom
- [ ] Work Ethic
- [ ] Working with Hands
- [ ] Working with Head
- [ ] Working with Heart
- [ ] _____
- [ ] _____
- [ ] _____

Blank Career Wheel

Directions: In the blank sections of the wheel add your top 8 Career Transition Values / Qualities from the previous assessment. For each section, circle the number that represents your current level of satisfaction in that area. The higher the number, the greater your level of satisfaction.

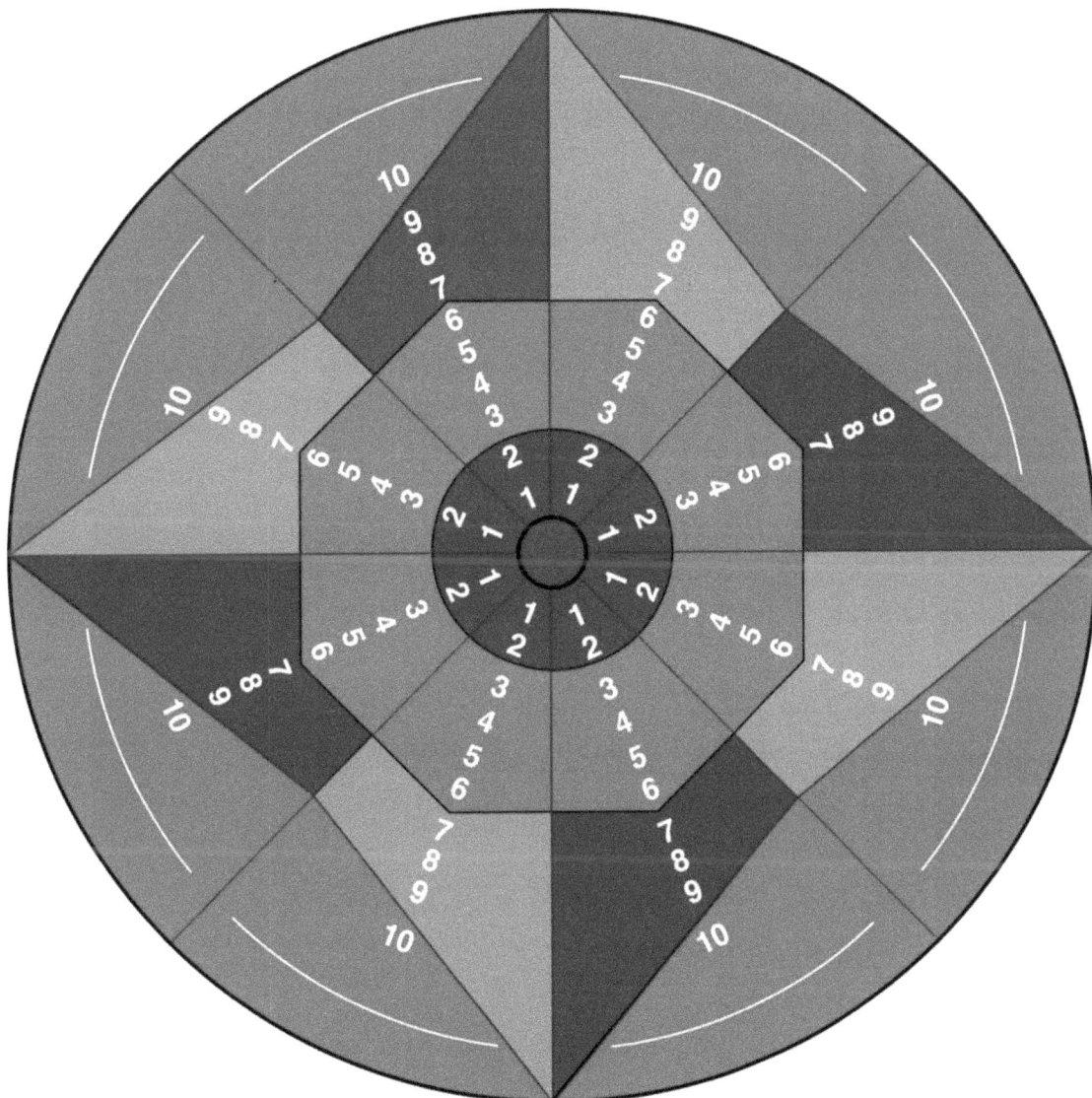

Career Transition Quotes

Your work is to discover your work and then with all your heart give yourself to it.
~ Buddha

For many people a job is more than an income — it's an important part of who we are. So a career transition of any sort is one of the most unsettling experiences you can face in your life.
~ Paul Clitheroe

Real success is finding your lifework in the work that you love.
~ David McCullough

Analyzing what you haven't got as well as what you have is a necessary ingredient of a career.
~ Orison Swett Marden

Never work just for money or for power. They won't save your soul or help you sleep at night.
~ Marian Wright Edelman

Everybody is talented, original, and has something important to say.
~ Brenda Ueland

Every man is the architect of his own fortune.
~ Sallust

The difference between a job and a career is the difference between forty and sixty hours a week.
~ Robert Frost

The best career advice given to the young is: Find out what you like doing best and get someone to pay you for doing it.
~ Katherine Whitehorn

What really matters is what you do with what you have.
~ Shirley Lord

It's not what you achieve, it's what you overcome. That's what defines your career.
~ Carlton Fisk

Creativity comes from trust. Trust your instincts. And never hope more than you work.
~ Rita Mae Brown

What is the recipe for successful achievement? To my mind there are just four essential ingredients: Choose a career you love, give it the best there is in you, seize your opportunities, and be a member of the team.
~ Benjamin F. Fairless

Three Rules of Work: Out of clutter find simplicity; From discord find harmony; In the middle of difficulty lies opportunity.
~ Albert Einstein

Think not of yourself as the architect of your career but as the sculptor. Expect to have to do a lot of hard hammering and chiseling and scraping and polishing.
~ B.C. Forbes

Try not to become a man of success, but rather a man of value.
~ Albert Einstein

A career is wonderful, but you can't curl up with it on a cold night.
~ Marilyn Monroe

In times of change, learners inherit the Earth, while the learned find themselves beautifully equipped to deal with a world that no longer exists.
~ Eric Hoffer

I think everyone should experience defeat at least once during their career. You learn a lot from it.
~ Lou Holtz

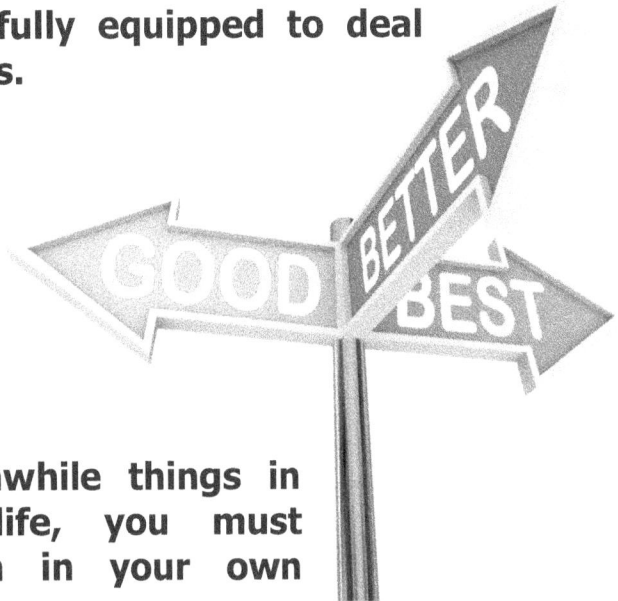

If you wish to achieve worthwhile things in your personal and career life, you must become a worthwhile person in your own self-development.
~ Brian Tracy

The test of vocation is the love of the drudgery it involves.
~ Logan Pearsall Smith

I cannot give you the formula for success, but I can give you the formula for failure: which is; Try to please everybody.
~ Herbert B. Swope

Don't ever let economics alone determine your career or how you spend the majority of your time.
~ Denis Waitley

Find something you love to do and you'll never have to work a day in your life.
~ Harvey MacKay

The price of greatness is responsibility.
~ Winston Churchill

Don't confuse having a career with having a life.
> ~ Hillary Clinton

Goals are dreams with deadlines.
> ~ Diana Scharf Hunt

No man can succeed in a line of endeavor which he does not like.
> ~ Napoleon Hill

Food, love, career, and mothers; the four major guilt groups.
> ~ Cathy Guisewite

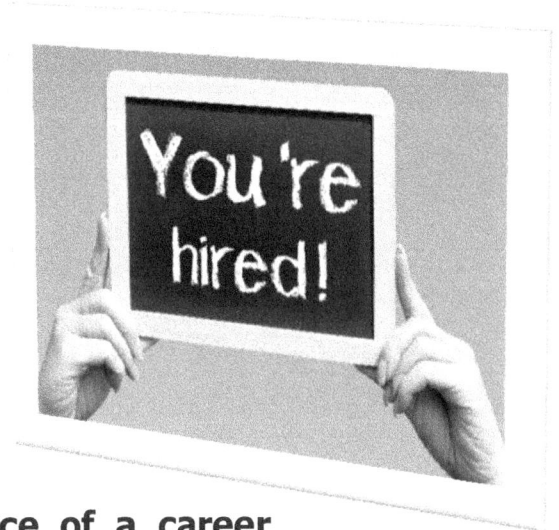

Job security is gone. The driving force of a career must come from the individual.
> ~ Homa Bahrami

A man who works with his hands is a laborer; a man who works with his hands and his brain is a craftsman; but a man who works with his hands and his brain and his heart is an artist.
> ~ Louis Nizer

Know what you want to do—then do it. Make straight for your goal and go undefeated in spirit to the end.
> ~ Ernestine Schumann-Heink

Give me a man who sings at his work.
> ~ Thomas Carlyle

Work and play are words used to describe the same things under differing conditions.
> ~ Mark Twain

Work to become, not to acquire.
> ~ Elbert Hubbard

To love what you do and feel that it matters—how could anything be more fun?
~ Katharine Graham

It is only when I am doing my work that I feel truly alive. It is like having sex.
~ Federico Fellini

People don't choose their careers; they are engulfed by them.
~ John Dos Passos

To find a career to which you are adapted by nature, and then to work hard at it, is about as near to a formula for success and happiness as the world provides. One of the fortunate aspects of this formula is that, granted the right career has been found, the hard work takes care of itself. Then hard work is not hard work at all.
~ Mark Sullivan

S.M.A.R.T. Goals Checklist

Specific

- ☐ What precisely is expected?
- ☐ Be as specific as possible.
- ☐ What will you have when the specific task is complete?
- ☐ What will the outcome be?

Measurable

- ☐ How would you know you have achieved success?
- ☐ How many tasks do you need to do?
- ☐ For how long?
- ☐ Make it a tangible process.

Achievable

- ☐ Is this achievable?
- ☐ What would be achievable?
- ☐ Do you have the skills or resources necessary to meet this goal?

Reasonable

- ☐ Is this a reasonable goal?
- ☐ What might be the obstacles?
- ☐ Considering everything else you have going on, can you achieve this goal?

Time-Oriented

- ☐ When will you be done?
- ☐ When will your tasks be scheduled?
- ☐ How long will it take to accomplish each task?
- ☐ When is the ideal time for this goal to be completed?

About the Work

We live in a time of great change. Faced with some of the most difficult challenges our world has ever known, we feel an urgency to find solutions to make our lives better. We want answers and we want them now!

In general, we focus on **getting the right answer not on asking the right questions.** Why is this? Perhaps it stems from an innate curiosity and a desire to make sense of the world. Perhaps it comes from a fear of the unknown or the need for a quick fix. It may also result from the need for blind acceptance of some *truth* where any form of questioning is strongly discouraged or denied. Perhaps we think we already have the answer, so why ask any questions at all? Whatever the case, there is no doubt human beings like answers.

When we focus on "getting the right answers," rather than "asking the right questions," we limit ourselves. We move into dualistic thinking: "I either have the right answer or I don't." We think in terms of yes or no, right or wrong, good or bad. **This black and white framework enables only surface inquiry**, at best, and quells deeper investigation and the ability to engage with others in meaningful ways. We lose the opportunity to generate new solutions to old problems.

Why are asking the right questions important? Because they generate beneficial lasting change. Empowering questions make possible diverse perspectives, which in turn lead to sustainable solutions to complicated challenges. They enable people to engage in dynamic transformational conversations out of which new ideas are born.

To generate the type of change our world needs, **we must raise penetrative questions to challenge current assumptions**; assumptions that keep us disempowered to affect change. The key in creating a positive, empowering future is asking positive, empowering questions now! So, what are you waiting for?

About the Authors

Kathy Jo Slusher, PCC, ELI-MP, Founder of Marketing Tao, LLC, has dedicated her life to help service-based socially conscious business owners make their business a success through sharing their passion. She believes that when your intention is on your passion and helping others, money is a natural bi-product. *It's not what you sell but what you stand for that makes you a success.* She is deeply committed to helping soloprofessionals and small business owners implement mindful marketing techniques and strategies to attract their ideal clients while making a difference in the world.

Kathy Jo is a Co-Founder of The REAL Results Coaching Exchange, partner in Coaching Skills for Leaders, a member of the International Coach Federation, and Vice-President of the United Nations Association of the US, Indianapolis Chapter.

Denny Balish, PCC, ELI-MP, Professional Certified Coach and Founder of ThreeFold Life Coaching, has dedicated her life's work to the development of Human Potential. She believes that each person has within themselves the desire and ability to be a positive force for change in the world and, by sharing one's unique gifts and talents with others, global change is possible. Denny is deeply committed to helping people and organizations get and stay powerfully on-purpose so they can be the change they wish to see in the world. Denny is a member of the International Coach Federation (ICF), Association for Global New Thought (AGNT), and founding board member of Spirit's Light Foundation, an alternative youth and family ministry with the Association of Unity Churches International.

Other Valuable Resources

For Coaches, Consultants, and Service-Based Small Businesses

Ultimate Questions Books

The real power in transformation is not in the answers, but in the questions we ask. If coaches, therapists or consultants are unsure of the questions to ask, client results are greatly impacted.

This series of books is specifically designed for coaches, consultants, therapists and others who are in a place where they need some fresh ideas to get themselves, a client, or anyone else unstuck. www.UltimateQuestionsBook.com

Marketing Made Practical

Marketing Made Practical is a Home Study Program designed for those who are overwhelmed with all the options and don't have a handle on how to make the marketing process into an effective, successful strategy.

Marketing Made Practical is specifically designed for service-based soloprofessionals or small business owners who are just getting started or have a limited experience and need an organized approach to marketing. www.MarketingMadePractical.com

Marketing Strategies University

Marketing Strategies University is an online training program that walks you through how to create a strong marketing and business development plan.

Marketing Strategies University cuts to the chase of marketing. We don't dive into the theory of marketing – but focus on practical steps to create and implement powerful marketing strategies.

This unique online training program is designed for service-based soloprofessionals or small business owners who have reached a certain level in their business where they are ready to create the systems and strategies for their marketing to take them to the next level of success. www.MarketingStrategiesUniversity.com

Marketing Strategies Success

Marketing Strategies Success is an online membership forum which brings together motivation and information into a community of like-minded business owners all working to create change through their business.

Through topic specific open Q & A calls & recordings, to an interactive forum where members share ideas, to a mentoring component of Success Stories, where successful entrepreneurs share their success secrets, this group will help those who have a message to share through their business but need marketing know-how & structure to accomplish their mission. www.MarketingStrategiesSuccess.com

For Leadership Development Support

Coaching Skills for Leaders

Employees don't leave companies, they leave managers.

According to the Gallup Poll, 71% of employees studied said they were either not engaged or actively disengaged at work. This employee disengagement results in $370 Billion lost annually. That's a huge amount.

In today's environment, talented individuals are arguably an organization's most valuable resource. Yet studies show, high potential employees have a higher turnover rate than any other employee population.

Leaders need to be flexible, adaptable, creative and resourceful to deal with the reality of our economic times. Coaching Skills for Leaders will take you and your organization through The Coaching Clinic, a specialized training program where you acquire a new approach to old issues. This process offers a step-by-step process of a coaching conversation in how to conduct & lead those difficult conversations. You will learn how to address organizational challenges through a step-by-step structured approach to facilitate your own coaching conversation, and develop partners and accountability standards across the board. Thus you will be transforming managers into true Leaders. www.Coaching-Skills-for-Leaders.com

Lifestyle, Leadership, Legacy

What are you working for?

As a business owner or executive you've worked hard to get where you are at. But how has this helped the lifestyle you want to lead? If you're tired to living to work instead of working to live, this program is for you.

We will identify your desired lifestyle, look at how to improve your leadership ability so you can more effectively lead those around you as well as your own life and create a lasting legacy to leave behind.

On-Purpose Leadership Development

For on-purpose professionals who want to develop their leadership acumen while expanding their consciousness. This program formulates a plan of action to break through all obstacles limiting your success, while building powerful skills to help you lead with purpose, including: manage conflict and chaos with greater ease, use your intuition for effortless decision-making, communicate effectively and persuasively, maximize your ability to engage and influence people in positive ways, and feel empowered to affect change in yourself and others.

For Specialized Support for Non-Profits, Social Enterprises and Cultural Creatives

Life Purpose Coaching

Empowering individuals in their midlife years to create a life of deeper meaning and purpose by not only connecting with their authentic voice and innate wisdom, but also by helping them aligning their skills, talents and interests with their desire to give back in meaningful ways.

On-Purpose Career Transition

For individuals in all phases of career and job transition who seek to purposefully align their skills and abilities with their passion for a satisfying career; one that enables them to give back in meaningful ways. Make a living while making a difference! This program is customized to fit individual needs.

For More Information Contact:

Marketing Tao, LLC
Kathy Jo Slusher
Email   info@MarketingTao.com
Call   317.536.5544
Click   www.MarketingTao.com
Click   www.TheREALResultsCoachingExchange.com

Threefold Life
Denny Balish
Email   info@threefoldlife.com
Call   708.209.6977
Click   www.Threefoldlife.com